SANKOFA
BLACK HERITAGE COLLECTION

HEROES

RÉGINE GRAND-PIERRE • ALISHA MOHAMMED

SERIES EDITOR • TOM HENDERSON

Ru'bicon
www.rubiconpublishing.com

Associate Publisher: Amy Land
Project Editor: Jessica Rose
Editor: Kaitlin Tremblay
Editorial Assistant: Kim Therriault
Creative Director: Jennifer Drew
Lead Designer: Sherwin Flores
Graphic Designers: Jen Harvey, Robin Lindner, Megan Little, Jason Mitchell

Every reasonable effort has been made to trace the owners of copyrighted
material and to make due acknowledgement. Any errors or omissions
drawn to our attention will be gladly rectified in future editions.

16 17 18 19 20   6 5 4 3 2

ISBN: 978-1-77058-946-9

We acknowledge the financial support of the Government of Canada through
the Canada Book Fund for our publishing activities.

Printed in Canada

CONTENTS

8

22

32

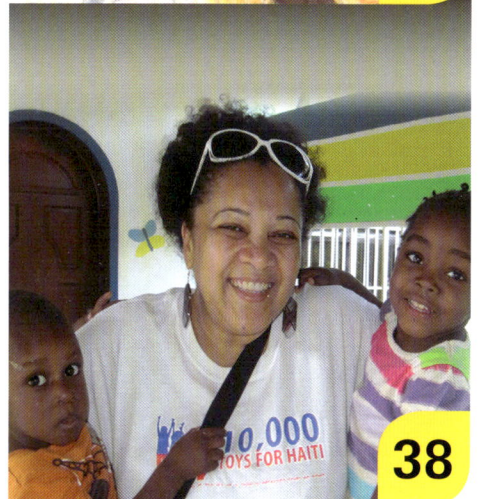

38

HEROES

There are many types of heroes.

A hero can be somebody in the past who stood up against injustice. A hero can be a modern-day activist or celebrity. An everyday hero is somebody who makes sacrifices for his or her family or community.

Some heroes are celebrated for their courage and bravery. However, many heroes go unrecognized. Every person we encounter has the potential to be a hero. Heroes are often ordinary people who do extraordinary things. They can inspire us to be better people. They can help us follow our dreams.

How do heroes make our world a better place?

WHAT IS A HERO?

What do you think about when you hear the word "hero"? Write a list of other words you associate with the word "hero."

READ THE FOLLOWING quotations about being a hero.

"An elephant that kills a rat cannot be considered a hero."

— African proverb

"I can accept failure. Everyone fails at something. But I can't accept not trying."

— Michael Jordan, professional basketball player

"Until all of us have made it, none of us have made it."

— Rosemary Brown, Canadian politician and first Black woman elected to Parliament

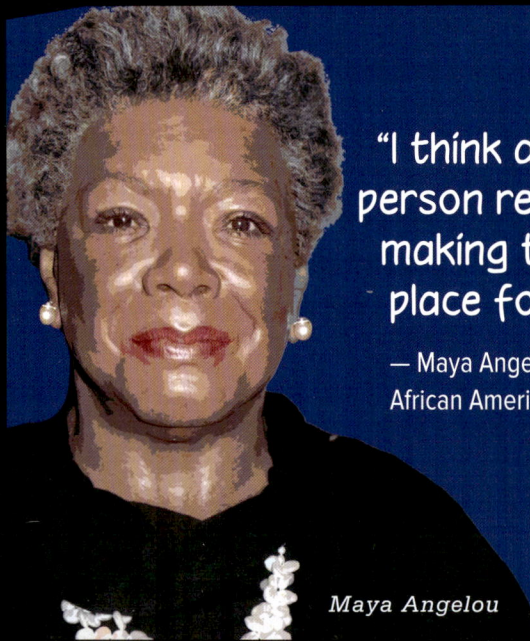

"I think a hero is any person really intent on making this a better place for all people."

— Maya Angelou, award-winning African American author and poet

Maya Angelou

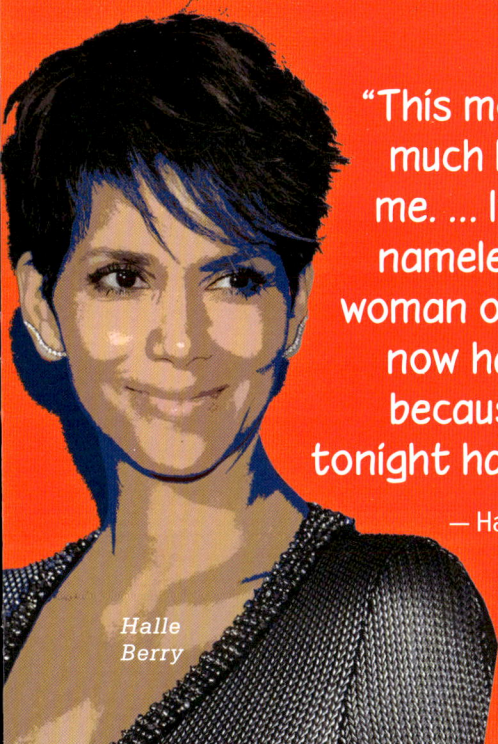

"This moment's so much bigger than me. ... It's for every nameless, faceless woman of colour that now has a chance because this door tonight has been opened."

— Halle Berry, on becoming the first Black woman to win an Academy Award for best performance by an actress in a leading role, 2002

Halle Berry

"You never want to meet the person you could have been, so never settle for mediocrity."

mediocrity: *state of being not very good*

— Jerome Singleton, American Paralympic athlete, recalling the best advice he was ever given

Jerome Singleton

"The thing about being first is that there are some people that take exception to you being there."

— Zanana Akande, the first Black woman to be elected to the Ontario Legislature, and the first Canadian Black woman to be appointed to a provincial Cabinet position

"We can love what we are, without hating what — and who — we are not."

— Kofi Annan, former Secretary-General of the United Nations, in his 2001 Nobel Lecture

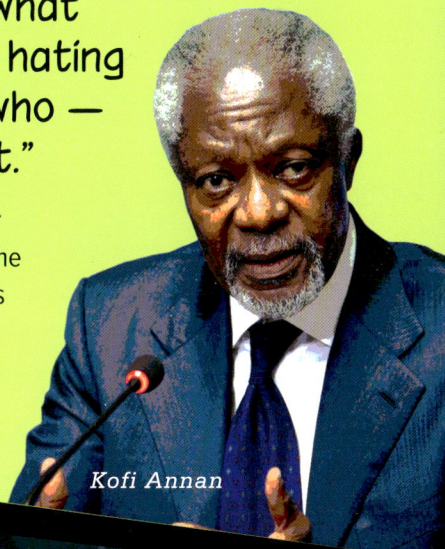

Kofi Annan

"True heroism is remarkably sober, very undramatic. It is not the urge to surpass all others at whatever cost, but the urge to serve others at whatever cost."

— Arthur Ashe, American professional tennis player

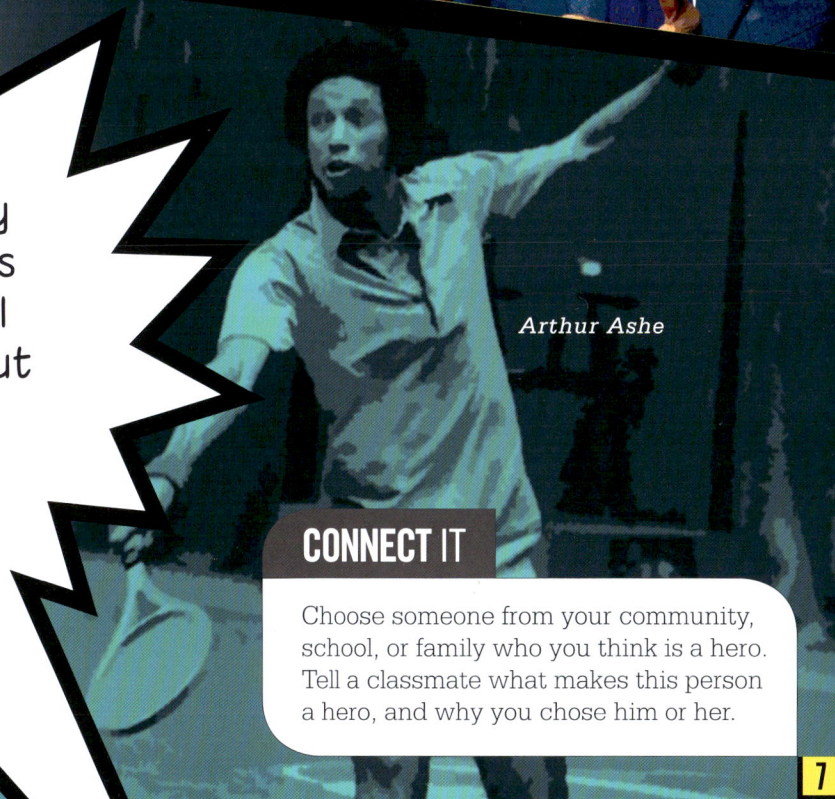

Arthur Ashe

CONNECT IT

Choose someone from your community, school, or family who you think is a hero. Tell a classmate what makes this person a hero, and why you chose him or her.

HEROIC MOMENTS

THINK ABOUT IT

Think of an important event in history, and a hero in that event. What makes this person a hero?

PEOPLE DO HEROIC things all the time. The following examples are just some of the many heroic events that have happened since people of African descent have been in North America.

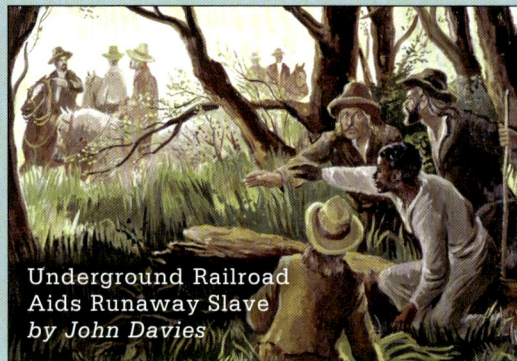

During an invasion by American troops in Lunenburg, Nova Scotia, Sylvia, a Black servant, helps her employer, Colonel John Creighton, while he is in the middle of battle. She brings him gun cartridges and musket balls, which she hides in her apron. After the battle, Creighton is rewarded for Sylvia's heroism and bravery.

Underground Railroad Aids Runaway Slave
by John Davies

Enslaved Africans escape from slavery by travelling along the Underground Railroad into Upper and Lower Canada. The Underground Railroad is a secret network of roads and safe houses that people escaping use to travel to freedom in Canada. Up until 1860, many Black and White men and women risk their lives helping those escaping reach freedom by helping them along the Underground Railroad.

Lieutenant-Governor Sir Francis Bond Head publicly praises Black Upper Canadians for their bravery and loyalty during the Rebellions of 1837.

1782

1812

1815

1838

1819

In 1812, the United States declares war on Great Britain. The British promise African Americans living in the United States freedom and land in Canada if they fight for the British against the United States. Because of this, many Black volunteers risk their lives to fight for the British — and for their own freedom.

James Douglas comes to Canada. He eventually speaks out against the slavery of indigenous people. His speech declares that slavery is a violation of people's "natural rights." He goes on to establish Fort Victoria, which later becomes the provincial capital of British Columbia.

indigenous: *people whose ancestors inhabited a country or region before people of other ethnicities and cultures arrived*

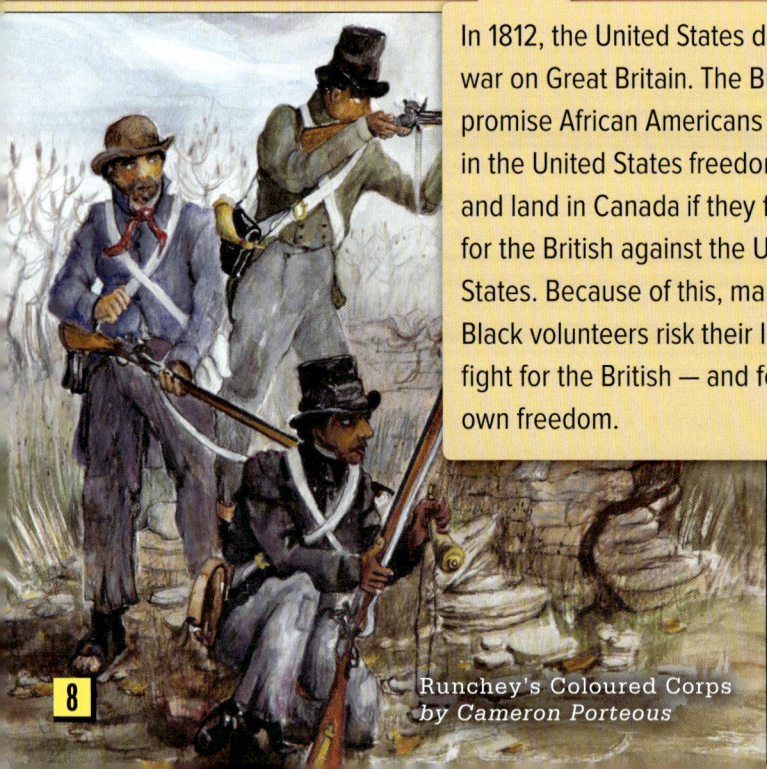

Runchey's Coloured Corps
by Cameron Porteous

in TIME

American abolitionist Frederick Douglass addresses a crowd of 1200 people in Toronto, Ontario. He discusses the evils of American slavery. Douglass was enslaved for the first 20 years of his life. His speech combats the stereotype that Black people are mentally inferior. After his death, the *Indianapolis Times* says that with his public speaking skills, Douglass proves that people of African descent are an "intellectual force."

abolitionist: *someone who works to end slavery*

William Neilson Hall, a member of the British Navy, helps defend a British fort that is attacked by mutineers in India. Hall climbs up the large wall of the Najeef Temple in order to help Britain overcome the mutineers. Hall becomes the first Nova Scotian and African Canadian to be awarded the Victoria Cross, an award given for exceptional bravery.

mutineers: *people, especially sailors or soldiers, who refuse to obey authorities*

Elijah McCoy, a Canadian inventor, is concerned with the high number of young Black workers who die while attempting to lubricate moving machinery on the railroad. He invents and patents a self-lubricating device that saves countless lives.

lubricate: *apply grease or oil to make something run smoothly*

1849

1851

1853

1857

1863

1872

Harriet Tubman escapes from slavery. She eventually helps nearly 300 enslaved people escape to freedom during 19 dangerous trips on the Underground Railroad.

Mary Ann Shadd starts a newspaper in Ontario, becoming the first Black female editor and publisher in North America. Her newspaper, the *Provincial Freeman*, argues for freedom and equality for all people. Before her death in 1893, she works as a teacher, publisher, lawyer, and abolitionist.

People of African descent who are enslaved in the United States play an important role in the American Civil War. They risk their lives as agents, spies, and scouts, bravely fighting for the end of slavery.

Members of the United States Colored Troops at Fort Lincoln

Women weighing wire coils

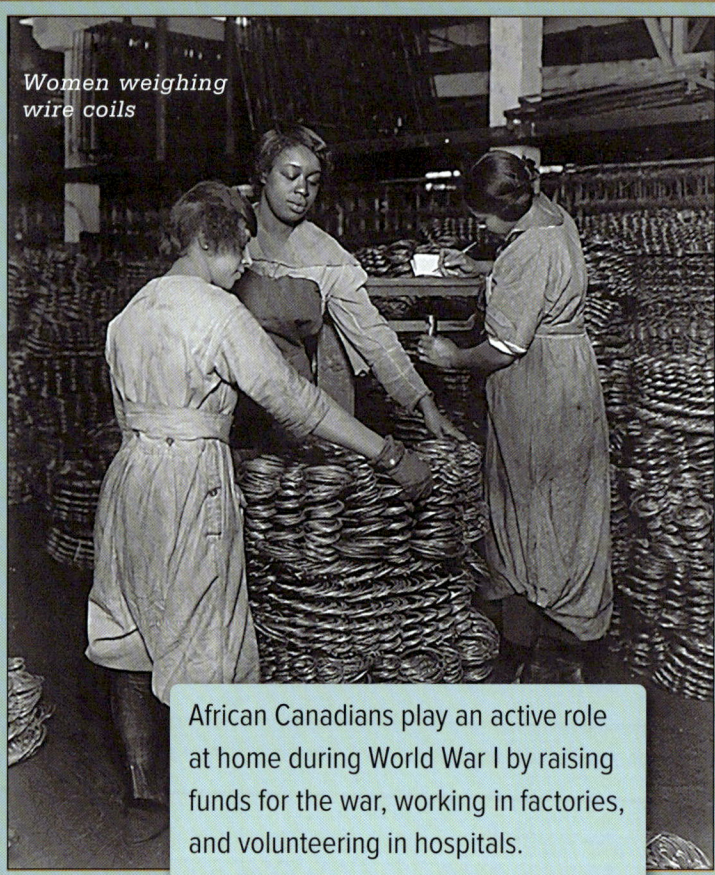

African Canadians play an active role at home during World War I by raising funds for the war, working in factories, and volunteering in hospitals.

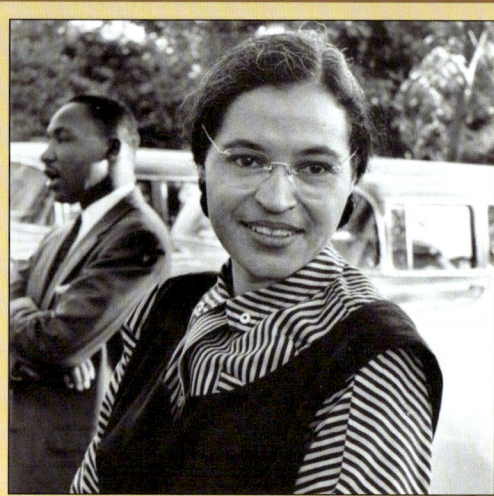

Rosa Parks refuses to give up her seat on a bus to a White person as the law requires in Alabama, United States. She is arrested. Her bravery and courage lead to a year-long bus boycott. Eventually, the buses in Alabama are desegregated.

desegregated: *no longer separated by race*

1914-1918

1909

1955

1939-1945

1963

The National Association for the Advancement of Colored People (NAACP) is founded in the United States. It is one of the most influential organizations working toward political equality, and equality in housing, employment, education, and transportation for all races. The NAACP is founded after the Springfield Race Riot, where White citizens assaulted Black citizens of Springfield, Illinois, after a Black prisoner was transferred there.

political equality: *everyone having the right to vote and to be treated equally*

Ida B. Wells-Barnett (left) and W.E.B. Du Bois (right), two founders of the NAACP

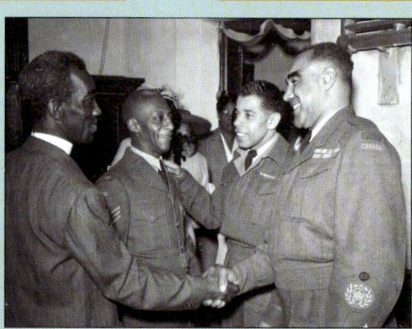

When World War II begins, African Canadians are not allowed to volunteer for the military. However, as the war continues, the military begins accepting Black volunteers. Although some segregated forces still exist, many African Canadians serve beside White Canadians.

Martin Luther King Jr. delivers his famous "I Have a Dream" speech in Washington, DC. This speech rallies people to fight against racism and inequality. Around 250 000 people attend. King dedicates his life to achieving racial equality. He wins the Nobel Peace Prize in 1964.

Josiah Henson 1789-1883
Canada 32
postage/postes

Josiah Henson becomes the first Black person to be featured on a Canadian stamp. In 1830, he escaped from slavery in the United States and founded the Dawn Settlement in Dresden, Ontario, for Black people who had escaped from slavery and for free Black people. He believed this settlement was a place where Black people could form their own community to help and teach one another.

Michaëlle Jean is sworn in as Canada's first Black Governor General. Born in Haiti, Jean had ancestors who had been enslaved.

Anthony Robles wins the NCAA individual wrestling championship in the 125-pound weight class. Robles, who was born with only one leg, wins with a score of 17–1. His opponent later says, "He just completely dominated me." Wrestlers usually depend on their legs to win matches. Robles's victory shows physical disabilities do not have to be obstacles to success.

1983

2005

2011

1966

2013

Rubin "Hurricane" Carter is convicted of a triple murder, despite little evidence. As a way of proclaiming his innocence, Carter refuses to wear the inmate uniform. He spends almost 20 years in jail. He is finally exonerated in 1985 when United States District Court Judge H. Lee Sarokin decides that Carter's "convictions were predicated upon an appeal to racism rather than reason." He moves to Ontario in 1988, where, until his death in April 2014, he works to help people who have been wrongly convicted.

exonerated: *found not guilty of criminal charges*
predicated: *based*

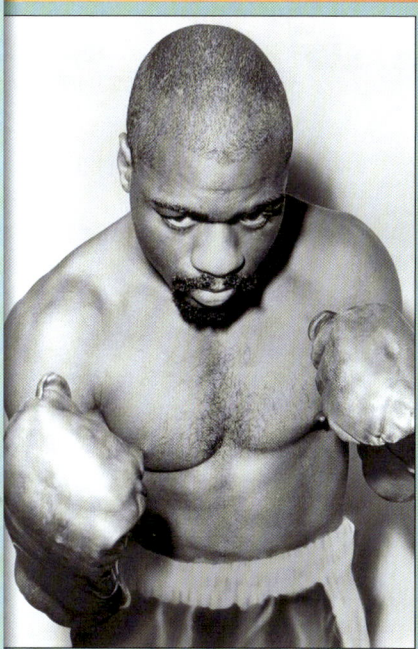

Djanet Sears speaks at the 2013 FemFest in Winnipeg, Manitoba. FemFest promotes social change and equal rights. Sears is an award-winning Canadian playwright who explores race and gender in her work. She is committed to preserving Black theatre in Canada.

CONNECT IT

Research an African Canadian who you believe should be included in this timeline. Write an entry to add to the timeline. Include information about what makes this person a hero.

A LONG WAY GONE:

MEMOIRS OF A BOY SOLDIER

BY ISHMAEL BEAH

THINK ABOUT IT

In a small group, talk about what you might expect to read in a memoir about a child soldier.

THE SIERRA LEONE civil war lasted from 1991 to 2002. In 2000, the international advocacy organization Human Rights Watch reported that children were being forced into combat during the war. Ishmael Beah became one of these child soldiers when he was just 12 years old. Today, Beah is an advocate for children's rights. He works hard to make sure other children don't have to go to war as he did. In the following excerpt from his memoir, *A Long Way Gone*, Beah writes about his life as a child soldier.

Ishmael Beah

ABOUT THE AUTHOR

Ishmael Beah was born in Sierra Leone. He was eventually rescued from being a child soldier, and he became a children's rights activist. In 2007, he became UNICEF's first Advocate for Children Affected by War. His bestselling memoir, *A Long Way Gone*, was released in 2007. In 2008, Beah co-founded an organization called the Network of Young People Affected by War (NYPAW).

When accepting his UNICEF role, Beah said, "It's just a way to give me more strength to continue doing what I've already embarked on, what I've dedicated my life to doing — which is to make sure that what happened to me doesn't continue to happen to other children around the world."

embarked: *started*

One of the unsettling things about my journey, mentally, physically, and emotionally, was that I wasn't sure when or where it was going to end. I didn't know what I was going to do with my life. I felt that I was starting over and over again. I was always on the move, always going somewhere. While we walked, I sometimes lagged behind, thinking about these things. To survive each passing day was my goal in life. At villages where we managed to find some happiness by being treated to food or fresh water, I knew that it was temporary and that we were only passing through. So I couldn't bring myself to be completely happy. It was much easier to be sad than to go back and forth between emotions, and this gave me the determination I needed to keep moving. I was never disappointed, since I always expected the worst to happen. There were nights when I couldn't sleep but stared into the darkest night until my eyes could see clearly through it. I thought about where my family was and whether they were alive.

lagged: *walked slowly; fell behind*

One night while I sat outside in a village square thinking about how far I had come and what might lie ahead, I looked into the sky and saw how the thick clouds kept trying to cover the moon, yet it would reappear again and again to shine all night long. In some way, my journey was like that of the moon — although I had even more thick clouds coming my way to make my spirit dull. I remembered something that Saidu had said one evening after we had survived another attack by men with spears and axes. Jumah, Moriba, and Musa were asleep on the veranda we occupied. Alhaji, Kanei, Saidu, and I were awake and quietly listening to the night. Saidu's heavy breathing made our silence less unbearable. After a few hours had gone by, Saidu spoke in a very deep voice, as if someone were speaking through him. "How many more times do we have to come to terms with death before we find safety?" he asked.

The names that Beah mentions in the following paragraphs are people travelling with him. All are trying to survive.

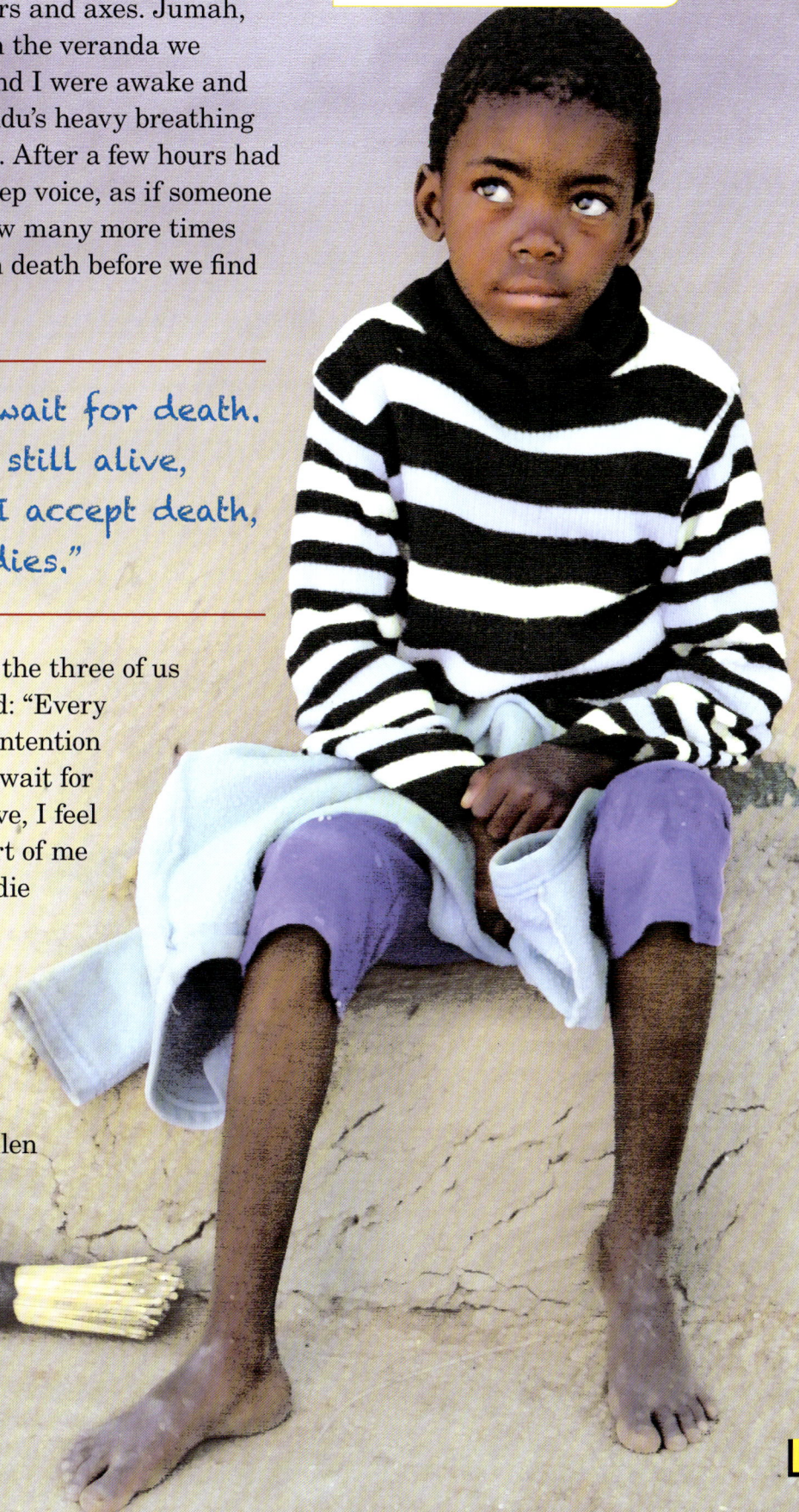

"I close my eyes and wait for death.
Even though I am still alive,
I feel like each time I accept death,
part of me dies."

He waited a few minutes, but the three of us didn't say anything. He continued: "Every time people come at us with the intention of killing us, I close my eyes and wait for death. Even though I am still alive, I feel like each time I accept death, part of me dies. Very soon I will completely die and all that will be left is my empty body walking with you. It will be quieter than I am." Saidu blew on the palms of his hands to warm them and lay on the floor. His heavy breathing intensified and I knew he had fallen asleep. Gradually, Kanei and then Alhaji fell asleep. I sat on a wooden bench against the wall and thought about Saidu's words. Tears formed in my eyes and my forehead became warm, thinking about what Saidu had said. I tried not to believe that I, too, was dying, slowly, on my way to find safety. The only time I was able to fall asleep that night was when the last morning breeze, the one containing the irresistible urge to sleep, saved me from my wandering mind.

Even though our journey was difficult, every once in a while we were able to do something that was normal and made us happy for a brief moment. One morning, we arrived at a village where the men were getting ready to go hunting. They invited us to join them. At the end of the hunt, one of the older men shouted, pointing at us, "We are going to feast tonight, and the strangers are welcome to stay." The other men clapped and began walking on the path back to the village. We walked behind them. They sang, carrying their nets and the animals — mostly porcupines and deer — that had been caught on their shoulders.

Upon our arrival at the village, the women and children clapped to welcome us. It was past midday.

The sky was blue and the wind was beginning to pick up. Some of the men shared the meat among several households, and the rest was given to the women to be cooked for the feast. We hung about in the village and fetched water for the women who were preparing the food. Most of the men had returned to work the farms.

I walked around the village by myself and found a hammock on one of the verandas. I lay in it, swinging slowly to get my thoughts in motion. I began to think about the times when I visited my grandmother and I would sleep in the hammock at the farm. I would wake up staring into her eyes as she played with my hair. She would tickle me and then hand me a cucumber to eat. Junior and I would sometimes fight for the hammock, and if he got it, I would trick him by loosening its ropes so that he would fall once he sat in it. This would discourage him, and he would go about the farm doing something else. My grandmother knew about my tricks and made fun of me, calling me *carseloi*, which means spider. In many Mende stories, the spider is the character that tricks other animals to get what he wants, but his tricks always backfire on him.

> Junior was Beah's older brother. Beah's parents and brothers were kidnapped when Beah was 12 years old, just before he became a child soldier.

> The Mende and Temne are the two largest ethnic groups in Sierra Leone.

Their faces seemed to be far off somewhere in my mind, and to get to them I had to bring up painful memories.

As I was thinking about these things, I fell out of the hammock. I was too lazy to get up, so I sat on the ground and thought about my two brothers, my father, mother, and grandmother. I wished to be with them.

I put my hands behind my head and lay on my back, trying to hold on to the memories of my family. Their faces seemed to be far off somewhere in my mind, and to get to them I had to bring up painful memories. I longed for the gentle, dark, and shiny old hands of my grandmother; my mother's tight enclosed embrace during the times I visited her, as if hiding and protecting me from something; my father's laughter when we played soccer together and when he sometimes chased me in the evening with a bowl of cold water to get me to take a shower;

my older brother's arms around me when we walked to school and when he sometimes elbowed me to stop me from saying things I would regret; and my little brother, who looked exactly like me and would sometimes tell people that his name was Ishmael when he did something wrong. I had trouble conjuring up these thoughts, and when I finally ventured into these memories, I became so sad that the bones in my body started to ache. I went to the river, dove into the water, and sat at the bottom, but my thoughts followed me.

After the meal, the villagers started playing drums, and we all joined hands and danced in circles under the moonlight.

In the evening after everyone had returned to the village, the food was brought outside to the village square. It was divided among plates and seven people ate from each plate. After the meal, the villagers started playing drums, and we all joined hands and danced in circles under the moonlight. During an interval after several songs, one of the men announced that, when the dancing had been exhausted, "whenever that will be," he jokingly said, "the strangers will tell us stories about where they are from." He lifted his hands and motioned for the drummers to continue. During the festivities, I thought about the biggest celebration we used to have in my town at the end of the year. The women would sing about all the gossip, the dramas, the fights, and everything that had happened that year.

Would they be able to sing about all that will happen by the end of this war? I thought.

I also wondered a bit why the villagers were so kind to us, but I didn't dwell on these thoughts, because I wanted to enjoy myself. The dance never ended that night and we had to leave early the next day, so we left as most of the villagers slept. We carried with us a plastic gallon of water and some smoked meat we had been given, and the old people we passed, sitting on their verandas, waiting to be warmed by the morning sun, waved and said, "May the spirit of the ancestors be with you, children."

When we were walking, I turned about to see the village one last time. It was yet to be born for that day. A cock crowed to dispatch the last remains of night and to mute the crickets that couldn't let go of the darkness of their own accord. The sun was slowly rising but had already begun casting shadows on the huts and houses. I could still hear the drums echoing in my head from the previous night, but I refused to be happy. When I turned away from the village, my travelling companions were dancing in the sand, mimicking some of the dances we had seen.

"Show us what you've got," they said, clapping and circling me. I couldn't refuse. I started gyrating my hips to their claps, and they joined me. We placed our hands on each other's shoulders and walked forward, dancing to sounds we made with our mouths. I was carrying the smoked meat in a small bag that I waved in the air to increase the speed at which we kicked our feet from side to side. We danced and laughed into the morning.

accord: *willingness; agreement*

CONNECT IT

What characteristics of Beah seem heroic to you? Do you think that he would consider himself a hero? Share your ideas with a small group.

I KNOW THE GRANDMOTHER ONE HAD HANDS

BY JAKI SHELTON GREEN

What does the term "everyday hero" mean to you? How is an everyday hero different from a celebrated hero?

OUR PERSONAL HEROES can be famous people in history. They can also be members of our own family who teach us our values and traditions. In this poem, read about a grandmother who is an everyday hero to her granddaughter.

i know the grandmother one had hands
but they were always in bowls
folding, pinching, rolling the dough
making the bread
i know the grandmother one had hands
but they were always under water
sifting rice
blueing clothes
starching lives
i know the grandmother one had hands
but they were always in the earth
planting seeds
removing weeds
growing knives
burying sons
i know the grandmother one had hands
but they were always under
the cloth
pushing it along
helping it birth into
skirt
dress
curtains to lock out
night
i know the grandmother one had hands
but they were always inside
the hair
parting
plaiting
twisting it into rainbows
i know the grandmother one had hands
but they were always inside
pockets
holding the knots
counting the twisted veins
holding onto herself
lest her hands disappear
into sky
i know the grandmother one had hands
but they were always inside the clouds
poking holes for the
rain to fall.

plaiting: *braiding*

ABOUT THE POET

Jaki Shelton Green is an American poet. She has a master's degree in community economic development. She uses her poetry to help others, including those living in poverty. She has hosted many workshops, including one called "Building Community through Poetry and the Arts." She lives in North Carolina.

CONNECT IT

Think of an everyday hero in your own life. Write this person a short letter explaining why he or she is your hero. Use some of your ideas from the Think About It activity when writing your letter.

Her Name Was Sylvina Bazilmé

THINK ABOUT IT

Write a list of things people who are older can teach younger people. Use examples from your own life if possible.

IN THIS PERSONAL ACCOUNT, Régine Grand-Pierre shares memories of her beloved grandmother.

Sylvina Bazilmé was my grandmother. She was my mom's mom. She was born and raised in Haiti. She raised her own five kids in Haiti. She finally breathed her last breath in Haiti, which is known as the "Pearl of the Caribbean."

I first met my grandmother when I was seven years old. Before that, I barely knew of her. I remember my mom showing me the only picture that she had of her mother. Looking at it, I immediately sensed that my grandmother was a sassy, but powerful, woman. She was barely five feet tall, and she had as many curves as the glorious Haitian landscape. In that crumpled picture, I could see that she exuded determination, resilience, and a sense of command.

In the photograph, my grandmother wore a traditional Haitian dress with a scarf. She had a hand on each hip. I couldn't help but wonder how someone who gave birth to my own mother, loved her, and raised her could be so foreign to me.

You see, I have visited Haiti only once, and that was years after my grandmother passed away. I met her when she visited Canada to meet my brother and me for the first time. My mother hadn't seen my grandmother in a very long time. As a young student, my mother received a bursary to study in Paris for a year. She met my dad, and instead of returning to Haiti, they moved to Montreal, where my brother and I grew up.

I remember the day my grandmother came to stay with us. She looked familiar, probably because she looked a little bit like my mom. She didn't speak a single word of French. She communicated solely in Creole, the language of "my people." I understood Creole, but when I spoke it, I sounded like a telephone call interrupted with static and silence.

---

exuded: *displayed; clearly showed*
bursary: *financial assistance*

My brother, who was only three or four, didn't know a word of Creole, but he rapidly learned under her tutelage. When I came home from school, I could hear them giggling together. They exchanged jokes. They formed a bond. I, on the other hand, shied away. I was awkward, and I just didn't know how to act around her.

Homework, for me, felt like a chore. I wanted to complete it quickly in order to do fun things, like listen to music or watch TV. As I worked, my grandmother paid special attention when I put pen to paper. I couldn't understand her fascination.

One day, as I was doing my homework, my grandmother seemed interested in what I was doing. She asked me to teach her to write her name.

My mouth remained wide open for a long time.

> My grandmother knew about setting goals, but most importantly she knew a lot about gratitude.

How can a woman who exudes such power, who has raised five children, not be able to write her own name? I thought to myself.

"How do you sign your name?" I asked her. She picked up a pen and a piece of paper. Without evidence of embarrassment, she handed the paper to me with a giant X written on it. In that moment, we finally forged a bond.

One might ask how we were able to communicate with each other. After all, we were two people who didn't share the same language. Actually, it was simple. We communicated through compassion. As I taught my grandmother to write her name, I felt tremendous compassion. She had

put five children through school, making countless sacrifices, without ever learning to write herself. She was a great example of a lifelong learner. Even at her age, she was ready to learn something new.

You might wonder how my grandmother lived for so long without being literate. You see, my grandmother was a hustler. Not of the criminal variety, but of the shrewd and clever variety. She sold livestock, fruits, and vegetables. After her visit to Canada, she also sold toothpaste, cheap sunglasses, scarves, and other objects that my mother and family friends collected for her.

My grandmother was a leader with a vision and dreams. Her dream was to build a house for her children and grandchildren in Haiti. Before she left Canada, she collected enough money to buy cement bricks to build her new home. She was an architect, a contractor, and a financing expert, even though she couldn't read or write. She counted her money, and spent it wisely.

My grandmother knew about setting goals, but most importantly, she knew a lot about gratitude. She was grateful for my mother, her other children, and her friends for making her vision come true through their donations of time, effort, and money. She was grateful for meeting my brother, who made her laugh. She was also grateful for awkward, seven-year-old me, who taught her how to write her name — Sylvina Bazilmé.

My grandmother was a hero. She taught me how to become resilient and grateful. Today, I am a teacher. She was a teacher, too. Her curriculum was the literacy of life.

In this sentence, "literacy" means "knowledge." What do you think the writer's grandmother taught her?

tutelage: *teaching; instruction*
literate: *able to read and write*
shrewd: *able to make good judgments*

CONNECT IT

Write a personal account about a family member or someone else you admire. Explain why this person is a hero to you. Include personal examples as Régine Grand-Pierre does in her account.

ENVIRONMENTAL HEROES

THINK ABOUT IT

Have you ever heard anyone ask the question "Are heroes born or made?" In a small group, discuss how you would answer this question.

THE INCREDIBLE WOMEN and men in the following profiles have all made the physical world we live in a better place with the work they have done to protect the environment. Read about their remarkable accomplishments in these profiles.

Wangari Maathai with her Nobel Peace Prize

A volunteer tends to a tree at the Green Belt Movement headquarters.

WANGARI MAATHAI
BORN IN 1940 IN NYERI, KENYA

As a child, Wangari Maathai loved to play outdoors and help with the work on her family's farm in Kenya. She also loved to learn, and later moved to Kansas, United States, to study biological sciences at university. She later earned a Master of Science degree from the University of Pittsburgh. Maathai then returned to Kenya, where she earned a Ph.D. from the University of Nairobi.

A lot had changed in her homeland. While she was gone, millions of trees in Kenya were cut down. This led to water and food shortages. People were suffering terribly.

Planting one small tree at a time, Maathai began to rebuild her beautiful country. She asked other women to plant trees and gave them the seedlings to do so. They did and, eventually, the land started to become green again. Maathai and her helpers started the Green Belt Movement (GBM) in 1997. GBM is an organization that empowers women both to conserve the environment and to help improve the lives of the people in their communities.

In 2004, Maathai became the first African woman to win the Nobel Prize. She was a professor, an author, an activist, and a mother. She died in 2011.

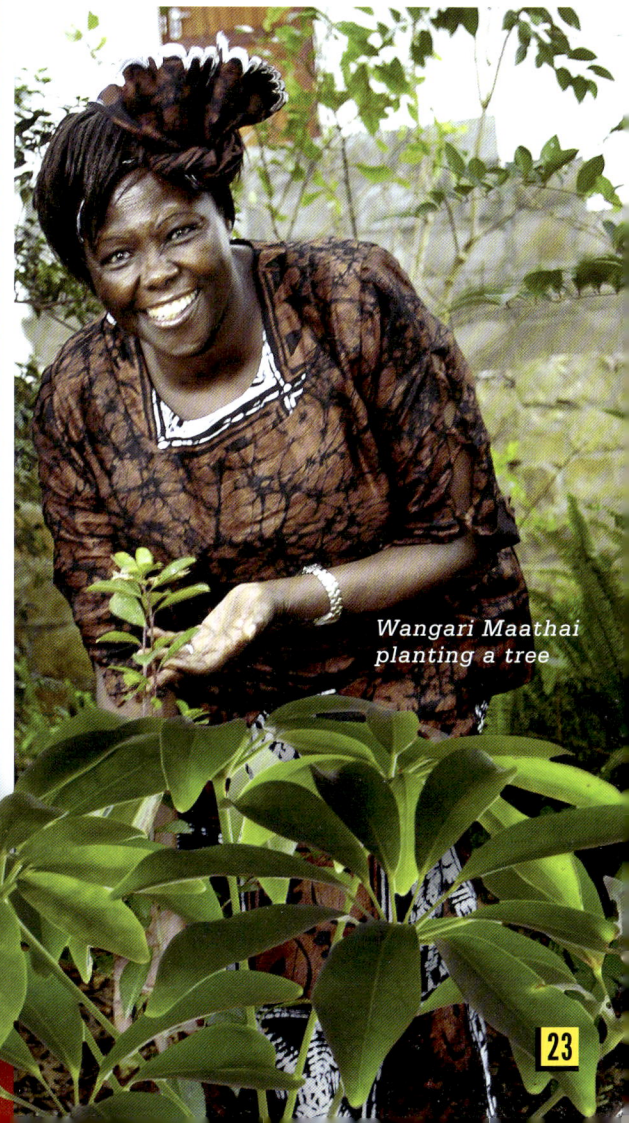
Wangari Maathai planting a tree

MARC ONA ESSANGUI
BORN IN 1962 IN OYEM, GABON

Ever since he contracted polio as a child, Marc Ona Essangui has had to use a wheelchair. But this hasn't slowed down his fight for environmental and human rights in Africa. Ona is the president and founder of the environmental organization Brainforest, as well as the president of Environment Gabon, a group of non-governmental organizations fighting for environmental rights.

In 2007, Ona exposed a deal that the Gabon government had made. This deal would allow an international company to mine iron ore from the Congo rainforest. The mine would include building a dam, which would flood the land and destroy the waterfall in the forest. Not only would the land be destroyed, but Gabon would receive only 10 percent of the profits from the mine. Ona fought to relocate the dam to a place that would hurt the rainforest less, as well as provide a greater benefit to the local communities.

For protesting against this mine, Ona was arrested and held in prison for five days. Of this, Ona says, "No matter how I was treated in prison, my resolve is unweakened. I think even, if I had spent 10 years in there, it is worthwhile to save what has to be saved." Ona received the Goldman Environmental Prize in 2009.

Marc Ona Essangui, winner of the 2009 Goldman Environmental Prize

William Kamkwamba

One of Kamkwamba's windmills

WILLIAM KAMKWAMBA
BORN IN 1987 IN DOWA, MALAWI

William Kamkwamba became a famous inventor when he was only 14. He hadn't even finished high school. Born in Dowa, Malawi, Kamkwamba grew up on his family's farm. In 2001, a famine struck, and his family's farm was badly affected. His parents were unable to pay the $80 school fee, so he had to leave school. Instead of giving up, Kamkwamba decided to work even harder. At only 14 years old, he read a textbook called *Using Energy* that would change his life.

Kamkwamba always had an interest in electronics. After reading about windmills, he decided to build one of his own. If the windmill worked, he could use the energy it created to power homes. His poor community could stop using expensive and dangerous kerosene.

Using only a broken bicycle, shock absorbers, and blue gum trees, Kamkwamba built a windmill. It worked! He used an old car battery to store the energy. He was able to power four light bulbs and even charge cellphone batteries. But Kamkwamba didn't stop there. He worked on many other projects. The projects included malaria prevention, solar power lighting for all of his neighbours, and a water well with a solar-powered pump.

Kamkwamba was finally able to go back to school. He has graduated from college, written and performed a play, spoken at several prestigious conferences, written a book, and even had a documentary made about him.

CONNECT IT

What is something you could do at home or at school to become more environmentally aware than you already are? Write a paragraph about what you could do and why it is important.

P.K. SUBBAN

IT WAS THE MOST SPECIAL DAY OF MY LIFE

LUKE FOX
SPORTSNET
6 SEPTEMBER 2012

THINK ABOUT IT

Why are athletes often considered role models and sometimes even heroes? Should they be? Share your ideas with a classmate.

SOME HEROES LIVE very courageous lives, fighting in wars or standing up against oppression in the name of human rights. But sometimes, heroes are people who put the needs of others first. These heroes sacrifice what they have in order to make somebody else's life easier or better. Karl and Maria Subban did exactly this for their children, sacrificing their time and energy to help their children's dreams come true.

P.K. Subban has never bought himself a car, even after the cheques from his $2.625 million NHL entry-level contract started coming in three seasons ago.

If it seems crass to begin a family story with money, then you don't know how money can change a family. How not having it can be a barrier between boys and their father's dreams. How finding a way to scrape together just enough of it can make those dreams as vivid as the colours red, blue, and white.

"The first car I purchased was for my father. I bought him a truck," Subban says. "I didn't want to see myself driving around in a nicer car than him. I wanted him to feel like he's accomplished a lot, too, which he has. He's put me in a great position." …

crass: *crude; ill-mannered*

"My family doesn't know what vacations are …," P.K. says. "A lot of my friends nowadays tell me they wished they could have played hockey, but their parents just didn't have the money. It's not easy. What my parents have done for myself and my brothers and my sisters is not normal. For a family to have five kids and to have emigrated from the West Indies, my father from Jamaica and my mother from Montserrat — it's not easy to provide for five kids, let alone put three kids in AAA hockey, one being a goalie, and put two daughters through university.

"It's unbelievable the amount of money that must've been transferred. My parents gave up a lot. They gave up getting their hair done and nails and going on vacation."

Karl Subban … was 11 years old when his family moved from Jamaica to Sudbury, Ontario, [to live] in a francophone community with decidedly colder winters and an ice rink at the end of the street. Despite their son falling head over heels for the Sudbury Wolves and Montreal Canadiens, Karl's parents couldn't afford to buy him hockey equipment or sign him up for minor hockey. His first pair of skates came from the Salvation Army, and he'd lace them up for outdoor shinny games and imagine he was Ken Dryden. But money prevented him from having a shot at becoming Ken Dryden.

So when Karl and Maria had their own children, the kids came first. And second and third and fourth and fifth. Raising their team in Toronto, Karl would drive his sons to the free ice at Nathan Phillips Square on school nights so the boys could skate, and he poured a home backyard rink to give his three puck hounds more ice time. When team fees, equipment bills, and travel costs mounted … , the Subbans fundraised by hawking tickets and chocolates at minor hockey games.

AAA: *highest level of minor hockey*
francophone: *French-speaking*
shinny: *informal game of hockey*

The Salvation Army (Sally-Ann in short) is an international charity that runs thrift shops and homeless shelters and provides humanitarian aid.

Montreal Canadiens defenceman P.K. Subban

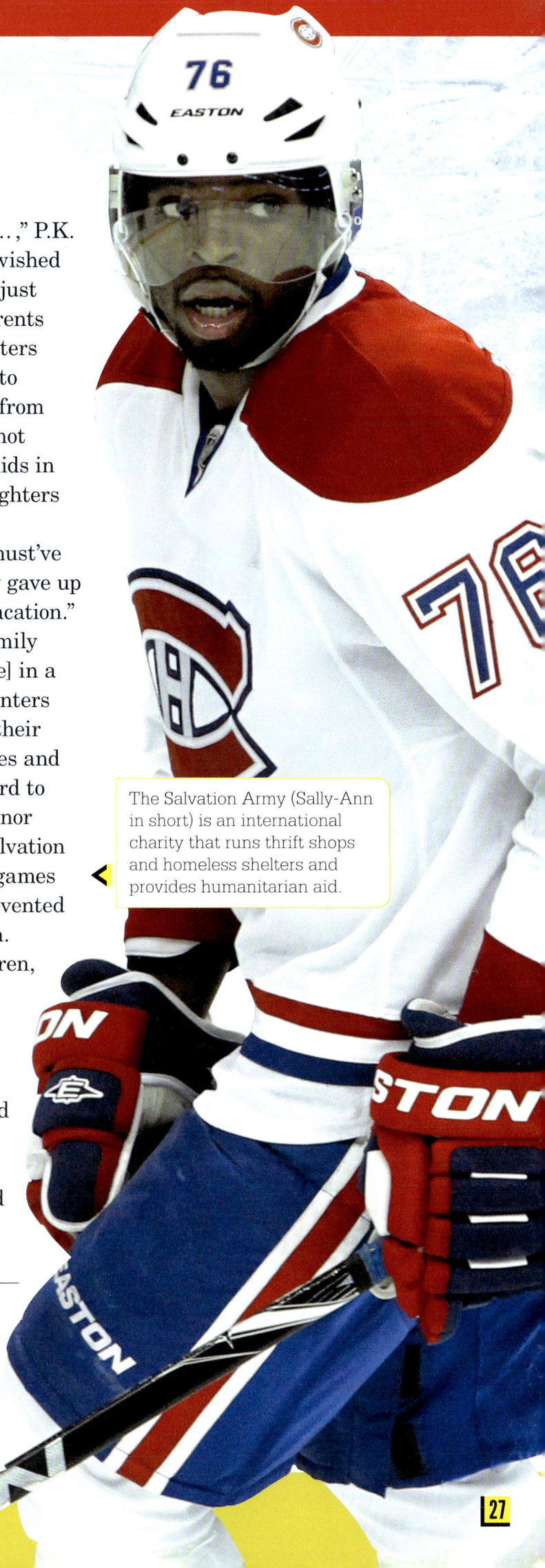

"We've made a lot of those sacrifices. Now I don't mind being able to send them on a vacation. This makes it easy to do those things, and I'm so happy to be able to do that for my parents," P.K. says. "But what they've done for us is unbelievable."

Malcolm, a goaltender, was drafted in the first round of the 2012 NHL Entry Draft by the Boston Bruins. He signed a three-year entry deal … Jordan, a defenceman, is a valued prospect who plays for the OHL's Belleville Bulls (P.K. and Malcolm's alma mater). He also won a gold medal with Canada's under-18 squad at this summer's Ivan Hlinka Memorial Cup.

> The OHL stands for Ontario Hockey League.

What should have been as probable as lightning striking thrice is now just a matter of time: all three brothers in the big league. P.K. doesn't buy that hockey lives in the Subban genes; when it comes to the nature-versus-nurture debate, he cuts hard to the latter.

"This thing about people being gifted – I believe people are [born] talented, but talent doesn't get you to the NHL."

"All three of us playing in the NHL is a product of us working hard. It's work ethic. This thing about people being gifted — I believe people are [born] talented, but talent doesn't get you to the NHL," P.K. explained. "You look at the best players in the game — Wayne Gretzky, Bobby Orr — they didn't sit on the couch and then one day join the NHL. They worked on their game. Their talent was perseverance, dedication. Those are talents to me; that's what gets you to the NHL.

"And through my family, we've learned about hard work and dedication. It's a trickle-down effect. It started with me, obviously, but now you can see it's working for my brothers. I've been harder on them than anybody else was on me, and they're going to benefit from that." …

The jersey P.K. wears today has number 76 stamped on the back, as usual, but [it has] Hyundai Hockey Helpers emblazoned on the chest. For the Subbans, ambassadors for a new youth program that launched this week, there will be no work stoppage.

ambassadors: *representatives; promoters*

"The work ethic hasn't stopped. We don't act like we've accomplished anything. We carry ourselves as if there's more to achieve, and I think this program is a start for that," P.K. says.

Hyundai and Canadian non-profit KidSport [joined together with the idea] of footing the hockey bills [full equipment and minor hockey league registration fees] for 1000-plus kids nationwide who otherwise would be restricted to Sally-Ann hand-me-downs and outdoor shinny.

"It's going to help thousands of kids get into hockey and play the game," P.K. says. "My only thinking is 10–15 years down the road, [seeing] one of these kids playing in the national league and thinking I was a part of that program. Like, *P.K. helped me get to the national league.* What a good feeling that would be."

Twenty-third June 2007 was a good-feeling day in the Subban house, to put it lightly. P.K. was selected in the second round of the 45th NHL Entry Draft by the Montreal Canadiens.

"He was in tears. He was really happy. He couldn't believe it; he was stunned," P.K. says of his father. "To have his son not only get drafted to the NHL but go to his favourite team … it was the most special day of my life." …

P.K. Subban participating in the Hyundai Hockey Helpers program

CONNECT IT

P.K. Subban and his brothers are heroes to many young people who dream of playing hockey. Choose one person who has a career you might one day like to have. How is this person a hero to you? Write a list of five questions you would like to ask this person about his or her job.

Akeelah
AND THE BEE

THINK ABOUT IT

Think about a time at school when you had to be brave. What was the circumstance? How did you feel before, during, and after?

AKEELAH AND THE BEE is a 2006 film about an 11-year-old girl who is a finalist for a national spelling bee. The director explained that the film was about "not being afraid of that thing you do the best … Own it and be proud of it and do it." Read this film review to learn why *Akeelah and the Bee* is an inspiring story.

Eleven-year-old Akeelah's life is not very easy. Her family doesn't have a lot of money, and her mother works all the time. Her older brother left to join the military. Her sister has a baby, and her younger brother is getting into trouble (and into drugs) with a local gang. Akeelah is very smart, but faces many obstacles that could prevent her from fulfilling her potential.

Akeelah tries to hide her intelligence from people at school. If the cool kids learn how easy school is for her, they'll bully her into doing their homework for them. Because of this, Akeelah needs some convincing from her principal before she enters the school spelling bee. She enters, and competes in front of the entire school. Winning the spelling bee is a breeze, and Akeelah qualifies for the Scripps National Spelling Bee, the largest and oldest spelling bee in the United States. This is when her quiet life gets turned upside down.

Keke Palmer as Akeelah

Akeelah and the Bee is heartwarming and funny, but sometimes sad. In the film, Akeelah faces many challenges. She doesn't receive a lot of support from her family. After the death of Akeelah's father, her mother is unable to support Akeelah emotionally. Akeelah has to face personal obstacles, racism, and other difficulties throughout the film.

Luckily, Akeelah is helped along the way by a mentor named Dr. Joshua Larabee. It isn't always an easy relationship. Dr. Larabee offers to help Akeelah with her training, but she is impatient at first. It's this relationship, along with a brilliant performance by actor Keke Palmer, that makes the film shine.

Akeelah and the Bee will be especially entertaining for younger audiences. As Roger Ebert says in his review, "I don't care if [young people] leave the theatre wanting to spell better, but if they have learned from Akeelah, they will want to live better."

With all its twists and turns, *Akeelah and the Bee* has a little bit of everything for everyone — and may just inspire you as well.

---

mentor: *experienced guide; teacher*

CONNECT IT

Choose a movie that features someone who could be thought of as an everyday hero, and write a review of it. Don't give away the ending, but provide enough details to let readers know if they would enjoy the movie.

Akeelah (Keke Palmer) studying for her upcoming spelling bee with Dr. Larabee (Laurence Fishburne)

JABU

SOMETIMES, MEMBERS OF your community may do something you think is wrong. Standing up for what you think is right is difficult, but important. Read about what happens when a young boy named Jabu comes face to face with a lion who has been trapped by hunters. This story is a folk tale from the Zulu people of South Africa.

There once was a young herdsboy named Jabu. He took great pride in the way in which he cared for his father's cattle. And his father had many cows — over 25. It was quite a task to keep these silly creatures out of trouble, away from the farmer's *mealies* (corn), and away from the dangerous roads. Jabu had some friends who also kept their fathers' cattle, but none of them had even half the herd Jabu did. And none of them were as careful as Jabu. It was a sign of Jabu's father's pride in his son that he entrusted such a large herd to such a young boy.

One day, as he sat atop a small *koppie* (hill) watching the animals feed and braiding long thin strips of grass into bangles for his sisters, Jabu's friend Sipho came running to him.

"Have you heard the news, my friend?" panted Sipho. Before Jabu could even answer, Sipho rushed on to tell him.

"Bhubesi, the lion, has been seen in these parts. Last night, Bhubesi attacked and killed one of Thabo's father's cows. The men of the village are already setting traps for the beast!"

and the LION

Jabu wasn't surprised by this news. His keen eyes had seen the spoor of the lion — his leftover kill, his prints here and there in the soft earth, his dung. Jabu had respect for the king of the beasts. And since Bhubesi's pattern was to hunt at night, when the cattle were safely within the *kraal*, Jabu had seen no reason to alert the village to Bhubesi's presence. But the killing of a cow! *I wonder*, thought Jabu to himself, *if the cow was left out of the kraal*. Thabo was known to be a sloppy herdsboy, a fellow who ran with his head in the clouds. He had been known to forget a cow or two before.

"*Woza, Ngane!* (Come, friend!)," Sipho urged. "Come with me to help the hunters who are setting up the traps."

Jabu slowly shook his head as he looked at Sipho and smiled. "You know me, friend," he returned Sipho's address. "I cannot put the cattle back into the kraal so early in the day. They need to be driven to the river before they go home."

Sipho smiled. "Yes, I thought you would say this. But I wanted to tell you anyway. I will see you later, friend, perhaps by the fire tonight." And Sipho ran toward the village with a final wave to Jabu.

Jabu had seen no reason to alert the village to Bhubesi's presence. But the killing of a cow!

Jabu began to gather the cows together. He waved his *intonga* (staff) and gave a loud whistle. Each cow looked up, and then, after a moment's pause, slowly started to trudge toward Jabu. With a grin, Jabu began to take them to water.

Jabu bathed his feet in the cool, refreshing river as the cows drank their fill. It was a fine, sunny autumn day, and, if his mind had not been so busy thinking about the lion and the traps the men were setting, Jabu would probably be shaping the soft river clay into small cow figurines for his young brother.

spoor: *signs; tracks; markings*
kraal: *enclosure*

Then, Jabu heard a sound that stole his breath from him.

"Rrrrroar!" came the bellow. The cows all froze, a wild look coming into their eyes.

"Rrrroarrrrrr ..." It was Bhubesi, and he was near! There was no time to drive the animals home; the lion was much too close. Jabu slowly rose, looking carefully around, his hand clenched on his staff. He walked purposefully, trying not to show the fear that made his knees tremble, pulling the cattle together into a tight circle. The cows trusted him and they obeyed.

"Rrrrroarr ... oarr ... oarr ... aaa!"

Jabu listened. Bhubesi was not declaring his majesty or might ... It sounded more like a cry for help. Several more bellows, and Jabu knew Bhubesi was in trouble. Somehow, this took most of the boy's fear from him.

Gripping his staff, Jabu quietly began to walk toward the lion's cry.

Yes, indeed, the lion was in trouble. Jabu found him in a small clearing several metres across the river. He was caught in one of the traps laid by the men of the village. His head was firmly wedged in the barred structure, and the more he struggled, the tighter the snare became. Jabu stood and stared. Never before had he seen the king of the animals so near. He truly was a majestic animal. And a large part of his heart was sore for the creature. Then, the lion saw the boy.

"Hawu! Mfana!" (Oh! Boy!) It is good that you are here. Please help me. I am caught in this trap, and I cannot free myself. Please, please, will you come and pull up on the bar that is holding my head here. Please!"

> What does Jabu's treatment of his cattle say about his personality? How does it make him a good member of his community?

Jabu looked into Bhubesi's eyes. He could not read them, but he could hear the desperation in the animal's voice.

"Please, Mfana! Please! Before those hunters come and kill me. Please release me!"

Jabu had a tender heart, but he was no fool. "I would very much like to free you, Bhubesi. But I am afraid that as soon as I did so, you would make me your dinner."

"Oh, no, *Ngane wami* (My friend). I could never eat someone who set me free. I promise, I really promise with full sincerity that I will not touch a hair on your head."

Well, the lion begged and pleaded so pitifully that Jabu finally decided to trust him and set him free. Gingerly, he stepped over to the trap and raised the bar that held the lion's head. With a mighty bound, the lion leaped free of the trap and shook his mane.

"Oh, thank you, Mfana! I really owe you something. My neck was getting so stiff in there, and I fear it would have been parted from my body by the hunters if you hadn't come along. Now, please, if you don't mind, Mfana, one last thing … I have become so thirsty from being in that thing, I would really like a drink of water. Can you show me where the river is? I seem to have become confused with my directions."

Well, the lion begged and pleaded so pitifully that Jabu finally decided to trust him and set him free.

Jabu agreed, keeping a wary eye on the lion, and led the lion upstream from where he had come, away from his father's cows, since Bhubesi had made no promise about not eating them. As Lion drank, he watched Jabu with one eye. He was thinking to himself, *Hmm … nice-looking legs on that boy. Hmm … and those arms are good-looking, too. Pity to waste such an excellent meal.* When the lion raised his head from the river, both eyes were on Jabu, and this time the boy could see what was reflected there. Jabu began to back up.

"You promised, Bhubesi," Jabu began. "I saved you from the hunters, and you promised not to eat me!"

"Yes," said Bhubesi, slowly walking toward the retreating boy. "You are right. I did make that promise. But somehow now that I am free, it does not seem so important to keep that promise. And I am awfully hungry!"

Gingerly: *cautiously*
wary: *suspicious; watchful*

"You are making a big mistake," said Jabu. "Don't you know that if you break your promises, the pieces of the broken promises will come back to pierce you?"

The lion stopped and laughed. "Hah! What nonsense! How can such a flimsy thing pierce me? I am more determined than ever to eat you now, boy," and he started stalking Jabu once more, "and all this talk is just serving to make me hungrier!"

Just then, an old donkey happened across their path. "Ask the donkey," said Jabu to the lion. "Ask him, and he will tell you how bad it is to break a promise."

"*He, wena!* (All right, you!) You are certainly dragging this thing out! So, I will ask the donkey." The lion turned to the old creature. "I want to eat this boy," he addressed the donkey. "Isn't that okay?"

Jabu broke in. "But he promised to let me go after I freed him from the snare," Jabu added.

The donkey slowly looked at the lion and then at Jabu. "I say," the donkey started, "that all my life these stupid humans have beat me and forced me to carry things. Now that I am old, they turn me out and leave me to waste away all alone. I do not like humans." He turned back to the lion. "Eat the boy!" and the donkey moved on.

"Well, that settles that," said the lion as he began to approach the boy once more. Just then, Mpungushe, the jackal, stepped between the two.

"I do not like humans." He turned back to the lion. "Eat the boy!" and the donkey moved on.

"Oh," he said. "Terribly sorry to have disturbed you. I'll be on my way …"

"No!" shouted Jabu. "Wait and tell the lion how bad it is to break a promise."

"A promise?" asked the jackal. "Well, I suppose it depends upon the promise, doesn't it? Why? Did one of you make a promise?"

Lion sat down and rolled his eyes up toward the heavens.

"Yes," Jabu said. And he told Jackal how he freed the lion from the trap, and how Lion promised not to eat him, and how now Lion was intent upon doing that very thing!

"Oh, what a silly story!" said Jackal. "My *nkosi*, the great king of all the animals, stuck in a little trap made by humans? Impossible! I don't believe it."

"It is true," said Bhubesi. "It is a strong and terrible trap."

"Oh, I can't believe anything is stronger than my king. I must see this thing. Please, will you take the courtesy before your dinner to show me this trap that you are speaking about? Please. Then, you can eat your meal in peace."

So the lion, keeping Jabu in front of him, led Jackal to the trap. "But you can't tell me that this little thing could actually hold your head. Never! I just can't imagine it. Nkosi, would you mind just sticking your head there so that I can see how you looked when the boy found you?"

"Hawu. You are taxing me with your questions. This last thing I will do for you, and then you must be on your way and leave me to my dinner in peace." So Lion stuck his head back between the bars just the way he had been when Jabu found him. Then, quicker than lightning, Jackal threw the top bar in place. Lion was caught fast once again!

"Yes," said Jackal, "now I see how you were trapped. What a pity that you are so trapped once more. But the boy is right, Nkosi. Broken promises always catch up with you."

Lion roared in anger, but the strong trap held him well. Jabu thanked the jackal and ran back to his cows, who were all patiently waiting for their shepherd's return.

Jabu drove them home and into the kraal. What a day he had had!

"Jabu, Jabu," Sipho said as he came running from behind Jabu. "The lion has been caught in the trap near the river! You and your cows missed all the adventure."

Jabu turned and smiled at his friend.

"We have had all the adventure we need for one day," he said. And as Sipho headed back to the hunters to hear the story once again of the mighty lion caught in the trap, Jabu greeted his mother in the cooking house and sat down with a sigh.

CONNECT IT

Choose a character in this story other than Jabu. Write a short retelling of this story from the perspective of that character. How might the story be told differently depending on the character who tells it? Who is the hero from this character's perspective?

Helping the Children of Haiti

THINK ABOUT IT

What are some ways that you and your school could help other communities in Canada that are affected by a natural disaster, such as the 1998 ice storm in Ontario and Quebec or the 2013 floods in Calgary?

WHEN THE DEVASTATING 7.0 magnitude earthquake hit Haiti in January 2010, Allison Harvey was safe in her home in Toronto, Ontario. She had never been to Haiti, and she had no friends or family there. However, that didn't stop her from doing all she could to help those in need after the earthquake. Read this interview to learn about her inspirational journey to improve the lives of Haitian orphans.

A girl by a row of tents that are still home to many Haitian families after the earthquake

Allison Harvey during a visit to Haiti

JACQUELINE L. SCOTT
ANANCY MAGAZINE
18 JULY 2013

Allison Harvey could not stand it — so many Haitian children were suffering after the 2010 earthquake. She gave a donation. That was not enough to satisfy her need to do something more. In a telephone interview, we talked about what drives her to help Haiti.

Jacqueline L. Scott: What made you start 10,000 Toys for Haiti?

Allison Harvey: After the earthquake, I felt I had to do something. There was so much need. It was hard to sit still and do nothing when so many people were suffering. I didn't know anyone from Haiti or in Haiti. But that was not going to stop me. I firmly believe that one person can make a difference. I started small, and now I have lots of connections in Haiti.

JLS: How many children have you helped in Haiti?

AH: Over the two years, we have helped about 2500 children in six orphanages in the Port-au-Prince area. Each year, we give them toys, backpacks, and school supplies.

JLS: When you go to Haiti, are they surprised to see that you are Black?

AH: Yes, they are! Nearly all the foreign staff of the relief agencies are White. They are helping, but it sometimes sends the wrong image of colonial times.

The Haitians are even more surprised when I tell them that I am a "Trini by birth and not by boat." They are happy to see someone from the Caribbean helping them.

Trini: *person from Trinidad*

What is the "wrong image of colonial times" Harvey refers to here? With this in mind, why is it important to have Black people helping other Black people in Haiti?

JLS: What is the link between 10,000 Toys for Haiti and HOPE Crossing Borders?

AH: 10,000 Toys is about giving charitable handouts. It has a role, but it is limited. HOPE Crossing Borders is the bigger vision. We want to build a transitional home for the orphans in Haiti. We want to create sustainability by teaching the orphans how to fish for themselves. Handouts encourage dependency. We want to build independency.

HOPE Crossing Borders is in the process of being registered as a charity. This means we will be able to give tax receipts for donations. We also want to be able to help other places in the Caribbean, and distribute our donations to all those in need.

HOPE stands for hope, opportunity, purpose, and edification. We want to live up to those standards in everything that we do.

> Even though the earthquake happened in 2010, HOPE Crossing Borders still exists today. Use the Web to find out what the organization is still doing to help the children of Haiti. How has it lived up to its standards of hope, opportunity, purpose, and edification?

JLS: How do you balance your life with the charity, your business, and your family life?

AH: I have always been busy. I have volunteered at lots of places, such as the Jamaican Canadian Association, the Leukemia Society of Canada, and the Jane and Finch Food Bank. It helps that my family is grown up, and they help me in everything. I also have a good group of friends.

sustainability: *ability to continue for a long time without being used up*
edification: *improvement of the mind and/or character*

Ms. Harvey was nominated for a GPHT Excellence Award in the Outreach Excellence category. This was in recognition of her hard work and contribution toward Haitians in Toronto and in Haiti. GPHT is the Groupe Professionnel Haïtien de Toronto.

Donations waiting to be sent to people in need in Port-au-Prince, Haiti

HAITI BY THE NUMBERS

7.0
Magnitude of the 2010 earthquake

300 000
Approximate number of people injured

80
Percent of schools damaged or destroyed

220 000
Approximate death toll

9.8 million
Population of Haiti

1.5 million
People left homeless after the earthquake

CONNECT IT

Research other people who have stepped up to help the people of Haiti. What have these people done to help? Write a speech thanking them for being heroes to the children in Haiti.

A SINGLE ROSE

BY MUSTAFA AHMED

THINK ABOUT IT

Brainstorm some practical ways that young people can be heroes in everyday life.

MUSTAFA AHMED USES the power of words to help break down barriers and inspire youth to be more involved in the world around them. Ahmed was only 12 years old when he wrote the poem "A Single Rose." In this excerpt of that poem, Ahmed inspires young people to pay close attention to the world around them.

ABOUT THE POET

Mustafa Ahmed is a spoken word artist from Toronto, Ontario. Ahmed grew up in Regent Park in Toronto, North America's largest housing project. He began writing when he was only 10 years old. By the time he was 17, Ahmed had already worked with Nelly Furtado, Broken Social Scene, and George Elliott Clarke. Spoken word is a performance-based form of poetry. It is focused on storytelling and the sound of words. He uses spoken word to teach others about important social issues. These issues include poverty, mental health, violence against women, cyberbullying, and education.

I will start by saying hi, hello, and my salute
And to my audience, please keep it down to a mute
People at the back, I hope I am pretty loud
And you back there; can you get in the crowd?
Listen,
I am not here to be line spitting
I am going to tell you the truth
And that's my real mission
And if u don't want to hear it
It's all right, you're forgiven
See, I used to be seven
And last year I was eleven
And I'm hoping that with the increase in age
Ears that actually listen surround me, as I stand on the stage
What I have to say
And my mission today
Is about the ridiculous injustices everywhere
About how most don't seem to be aware
About the different avenues to help out there
About how we can start by showing we care ...
About
The fact that their cries, and tears
Are so loud
And clear
That I fear
How our hearts appear
When we all hear
Their sincere
And severe
Pain
That disappears
As we strive for our own lives' gain
But all we do is ignore
And store
All the thoughts in our head
We see people starving on the street
Beat
Hopes defeat
Wishes delete
Opportunities fleet
Happiness a deceit
But why do people have to live in fear
Why do people have to assume that death is near?
And are you guys finally starting to hear ...
And so my dream is to raise awareness
For those who care
About the injustices
Out there
Can't we spare?

Some time
And share
A lifeline
And let people know that life doesn't have to be a nightmare
Do you guys understand?
That I don't have to be a religious man
To recognize the injustices in the elites' plan ◀
Do you guys understand (yes?)
Then why is life still such a mess
Why do people still have to live in stress?
It's like when you're playing chess
Your strategy
Determines if you are the best
And my strategy
Is to reach out to anyone's hand
At least,
Show them that I'm willing to understand
What's yours?
Remember, last year I was eleven
Not seven
Don't let me be a single rose, with this big dream, in this run down park.

---

fleet: *move very quickly*
deceit: *dishonesty*

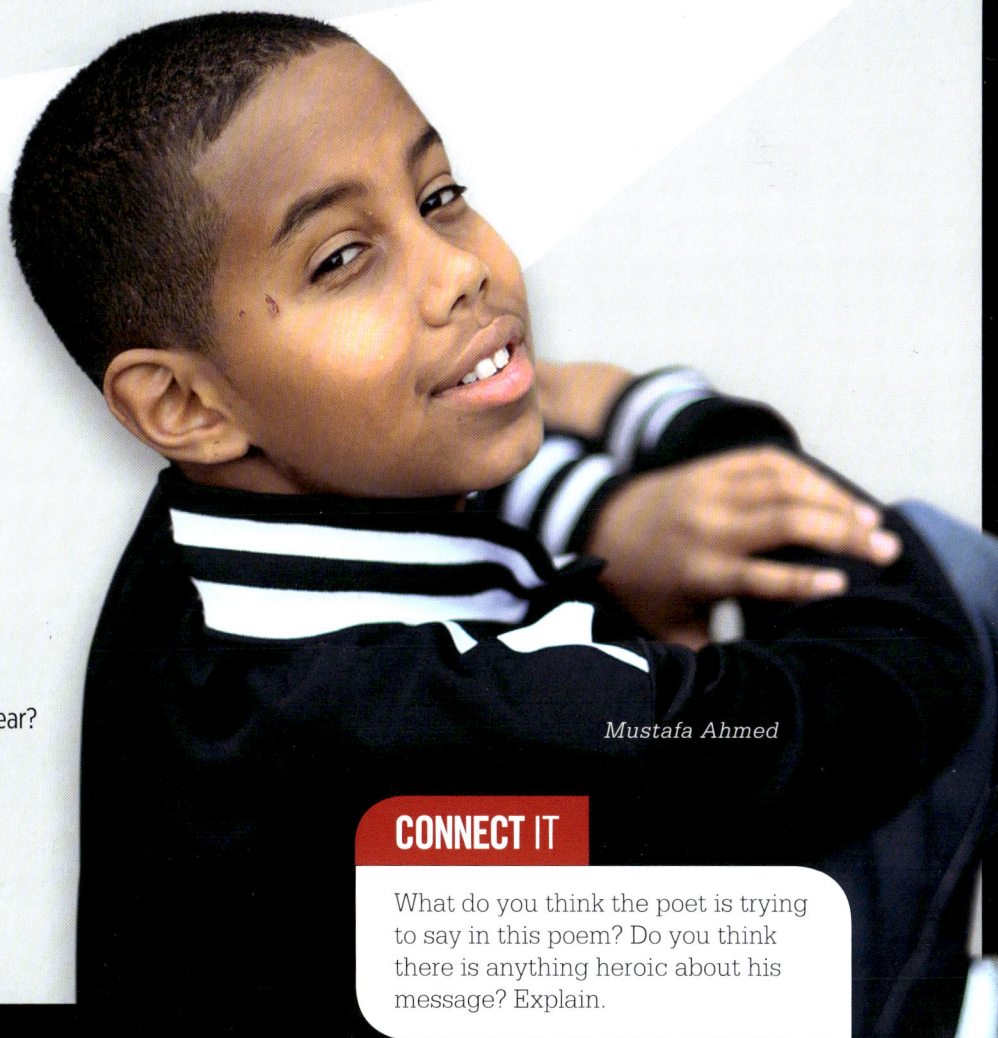

> Ahmed is talking about wealthy, powerful people not treating others equally. List some examples you see of people not being treated equally.

Mustafa Ahmed

CONNECT IT

What do you think the poet is trying to say in this poem? Do you think there is anything heroic about his message? Explain.

THE
IMPORTANCE
OF DIFFERENCE MAKERS

THINK ABOUT IT

Think about a time when someone made a difference in your life. What did he or she do? How did it make you feel?

WINNIPEG'S CHIEF OF POLICE Devon Clunis is a present-day hero. Born in Jamaica, Clunis immigrated to Canada in 1975 at the age of 12 with his family. Transitioning to his new life in Canada had its challenges. He failed grade 6, but with the support of a caring teacher, he eventually became successful. Since then, he has spent his life working to become what he calls a "difference maker."

To be a difference maker is to be a hero. It is someone who finds a purpose, has a desire to make a difference, and sets out to make change happen. Clunis set out to make a difference in the lives of Black youth by setting an example and working against the stereotypes that surround young Black men. Clunis has become a difference maker and hero to Canada's Black community — and indeed to all Canadians. To learn more about him, read the following speech he gave at a reception on 5 February 2013 at the Black History Month launch in Ottawa, Ontario.

Transitioning: *adapting; changing*

Thank you. I truly was humbled when I received the call asking me to attend this event. I thought, "Why me, truly?" I don't feel I'm anyone special. I have to tell you honestly that, when I became a police officer, I did not set out to make any type of history. I simply set out to make a difference by impacting the lives of young people in a positive way, the same way my life had been impacted.

I was initially driven by a desire to set an example for Black youth in our city, to break the stereotypes seen in mainstream media of what it meant to be Black. I soon realized that the need for role models crossed ethnic boundaries, and that the youth didn't care what you looked like, as long as you cared about them.

The main message I want to leave you with in the brief time we have together is that, when given the opportunity, we have a responsibility to be a difference maker, particularly in the lives of young people.

"In this very moment, I'm continuing to live my dream, my desire for making a difference."

Our ability to be difference makers is not dependent on our occupation, it's certainly not dependent on our ancestry, it's not dependent on our social status or any other limitations individuals or society may try to place on us. We simply need to make that our purpose, our driving desire, to make a difference, and set out to find a way.

In this very moment, I'm continuing to live my dream, my desire for making a difference.

I'm driven by the experiences of a little boy who immigrated to Canada in 1975, unsure of what the future had in store for him.

A little boy who was challenged by cultural upheaval, a little boy who was able to succeed because individuals purposefully set out to make a difference in his life.

---

cultural upheaval: *major change in the culture (beliefs, way of life, etc.) of a society; major change in one's surroundings*

I always honour my mother as the first difference maker in my life because of her courage and sacrifice to leave our homeland of Jamaica to find a new life in Canada. That took tremendous courage.

But teachers significantly impacted my life as well. The little boy in grade 6, as I told you, struggled initially with the changes — not only the weather, but the cultural upheaval. I failed grade 6.

> **"But because those teachers dedicated their time, they made a difference and my life stayed on the straight and narrow."**

A teacher, Mrs. Hannah — I'll always remember her. She said, "Devon, if you would come to school an hour early every day, I'll meet you." So I would faithfully get up every day, and I would join Mrs. Hannah an hour ahead of all the kids. And three years later, the little boy who failed grade 6, with a teacher who dedicated time and effort to him, graduated grade 9 as the top student in his school because she made a difference.

I remember being in high school and playing basketball and being involved in sports, and I would see these teachers who would dedicate so much of their extra time to be with us as young men and, I say, basically kept us on the straight and narrow, because there were lots of opportunities to find ourselves doing the wrong thing. But because those teachers dedicated their time, they made a difference and my life stayed on the straight and narrow.

These individuals made a difference, and as I came of age and began to understand life, I wanted to be like them. I wanted to give back and make a difference.

As a young person, I was profoundly aware of the depiction of Blacks and other minorities in mainstream media. The stereotypical roles assigned to minorities were those of the "the bad guy, the less desirable."

depiction: *representation*

Minister of Children and Youth Opportunities Kevin Chief (left) and Devon Clunis (right) lead Norquay School students in activities.

We know that young people can clothe themselves with damaging images manufactured by pop culture. My image of who we are as people of colour was *solidified* when I watched the pivotal miniseries *Roots*. I was in grade 9.

Kids would tease me by calling me "Kunta Kinte," the young African slave who was captured and brought to America. In spite of what he suffered, Kunta Kinte maintained his sense of pride and dignity. He refused to be broken.

As I watched that miniseries, the thing that dawned on my grade 9 mind was "Wow, we are a strong people. If we can survive that and still be here, I have a lot to be proud of."

I remembered thinking to myself, we don't always have to be "the bad guy," and I set out to *exemplify* that in my life. I determined I would do something to set an example for other children to follow.

I've been blessed to have the opportunity to live this dream. I've been part of mentorships programs for youth of all ethnic backgrounds in our city.

It is important to celebrate the accomplishments and contributions of Black Canadians. It helps to counter some of the negative portrayals we still see in popular culture and [to] help young people *envision* an alternate future.

We live in a great country. I live in one of the most ethnically diverse cities within this great country.

More than ever, Canada is a nation of immigrants. Cultural diversity is the strength and future of our country.

So my hope is this: that each person here will determine to be that difference maker in ensuring that everyone living within this amazing, amazing country, this *cultural mosaic*, has the opportunity to contribute to the continued health and welfare of our country.

If not for those difference makers, I would not be here today. Let's each and every single one of us determine to be a difference maker in the future of our country.

Thank you.

---

solidified: *made stronger*
exemplify: *serve as an example of*
envision: *imagine*
cultural mosaic: *mix of people of different languages, backgrounds, and cultures that live together in a society*

CONNECT IT

Do you think it is more important to help out globally or within your own community? Why? Brainstorm some of the most effective ways you could make a difference today in either the world or your community.

Index

Acknowledgements

Beah, Ishmael. Excerpt from *A Long Way Gone: Memoirs of a Boy Soldier*. Copyright © 2007 by Ishmael Beah. Reprinted by permission of Farrar, Straus and Giroux, LLC.

Clunis, Devon. "The Importance of Difference Makers." Speech delivered on 5 February 2013 at the Black History Month 2013 Launch Reception in Ottawa, Ontario. Reprinted with permission of Chief of Police Devon Clunis, Winnipeg Police Service.

Fox, Luke. "P.K.: 'It Was the Most Special Day of My Life'," from *Sportsnet* magazine, 6 September 2012. Reprinted with permission.

Green, Jaki Shelton. "I know the grandmother one had hands," originally published in *Breath of the Song: New and Selected Poems* by Jaki Shelton Green. Carolina Wren Press, 2005. Permission courtesy of Carolina Wren Press.

Mustafa the Poet. "A Single Rose." Reprinted by permission of Dream Machine.

Scott, Jacqueline L. "Helping the Children of Haiti," from *Anancy Magazine*, 18 July 2013. © ANANCY MAGAZINE 2013. All rights reserved. Reprinted with permission.

Photo Sources

Cover: [doctor–sireoni; lady–michaeljun; officer–Alan Poulson Photograph] Shutterstock.com; **4:** superhero–Malchev/Shutterstock.com; **6:** [basketball–heromen30; Maya Angelou–JStone] Shutterstock.com; **7:** Halle Barry–Dfree/Shutterstock.com; Jerome Singleton–Jim Cowsert-USA TODAY Sports; Kofi Annan–United States Mission Geneva; Arthur Ashe–Bogaerts, Rob / Anefo; **8:** background–barbaliss/Shutterstock.com; Underground Railroad–painting by John Davies/SuperStock/Glow; Sir Francis Bond Head–Nelson Cook, C. Turner; Runchey's Coloured Corps–canadianartcards.com; **9:** Frederick Douglass; William Hall; Harriet Tubman; troops–Library of Congress; Elijah McCoy–uspto.gov; Mary Ann Shadd–Library and Archives Canada; **10:** working women–National Archives Canada; Ida B. Wells-Barnett–Mary Garrity; W.E.B. Du Bois–Library of Congress; Rosa Parks– National Archives and Records Administration

Records of the U.S. Information Agency Record Group 306; volunteers–John Boyd/City of Toronto Archives; Martin Luther King Jr.– Library of Congress; **11:** Josiah Henson–rook76/Shutterstock.com; Michaëlle Jean–Agência Brasil; Hurricane Carter–Everett Collection/Superstock; Djanet Sears–courtesy of Djanet Sears; **12:** [clouds–ffolas; village–Luke Schmidt; desert–Julija Sapic] Shutterstock.com; Ishmael Baeh–Keith Beaty / GetStock.com; **13:** boy–Lucian Coman/Shutterstock.com; **14:** crowd–Klemen Misic/Shutterstock.com; **15:** scene–Lucian Coman/Shutterstock.com; **16:** dancing–Hector Conesa–Shutterstock.com; **17:** running–Sam Dcruz/Shutterstock.com; **18:** hands–iStockphoto.com/ © alaincouillaud; flowers–anemad/Shutterstock.com; **19:** Jaki Shelton Green–courtesy of Jaki Shelton Green; **20:** [paper–Ivankov; wicker–kmintstock] Shutterstock.com; writing–Blend Images / SuperStock; **22:** [earth–musicman; hand–photka] Shutterstock.com; **23:** trees–giulio napolitano/Shutterstock.com; Wangari Maathai–EPA/Bendiksby/Newscom; Kario Wanae–TONY KARUMBA / Stringer / Getty Images; Wangari Maathai–GIANLUIGI GUERCIA / Stringer / Getty Images; **24:** Marc Ona Essangui–International Rivers; **25:** windmill background–Tom Rielly; William Kamkwamba–Bobby Longoria / Contributor / Getty Images; **26:** [ice background–kaarsten; hockey stick–Flashon Studio] Shutterstock.com; P.K. Subban–Kim Klement-USA TODAY Sports; **28:** [puck–B Calkins; puck–Lindsay Douglas] Shutterstock.com; Hyundai Helper program–Hand-out/HYUNDAI AUTO CANADA CORP./Newscom; **30:** [background–Feaspb; star–Feaspb] Shutterstock.com; Akeelah–Entertainment Pictures/Keystone; **31:** letters–avian/Shutterstock.com; movie scene–Entertainment Pictures/Keystone; **32:** lion prints–Villiers Steyn; cattle background–WOLF AVNI/ Shutterstock.com; **33:** illustrations–Jen Harvey; **34:** [cattle–Dennis W. Donohue; lion–Thomas Barrat] Shutterstock.com; **35:** lion–Sergey Uryadnikov/Shutterstock.com; **36:** [lion–Eric Isselee; jackal–Eric Isselee] Shutterstock.com; **37:** [lion–Pablo77; cattle–Sam Dcruz] Shutterstock.com; **38:** girl–Reynold Mainse / Design Pics / SuperStock; **39:** Allison Harvey–courtesy of Allison Harvey; **40:** donation packages–Lance Cpl. Christopher M. Carrol/US Marines Website; **41:** [grunge frame–Gordan; globe–AridOcean] Shutterstock.com; **42:** [asphalt–bahri altay; rose–Alesikka] Shutterstock.com; **43:** Mustafa Ahmed–Tara Walton / GetStock.com; **44:** Devon Clunis–Wayne Glowacki/Winnipeg Free Press; **45:** concrete texture–praet/Shutterstock.com; **46:** basketball players–S.Pytel/Shutterstock.com; **47:** Run with the Chiefs–Jessica Burtnick/Winnipeg Free Press.